Resurrection

~ Mark Loiselle ~

From weeping skies, a fallen angel spills,
Unfurling wings, escaping heaven's hills.
Her reign once mighty in the halls of hell,
Now tears betray the sorrow she can't quell.

She cherished life, embraced each fleeting breath,
Shielding us from shadows, pain, and death.
More than mere holiness, a vibrant soul,
With boundless love that makes us whole.

No earthly cause explains the sudden blow,
The lightning's flash that brought her down below.
She gave her spirit freely, this we know,
A tapestry of starlight she would sew.

Where once we saw a fall, a sinful plight,
Now love illuminates her endless flight.

Neopoet Around The Globe

Anthology

Third Edition

Produced by Neopoet.com Anthology Group

Neopoet Around the Globe

Neopoet

Volume three

Table of Contents

Welcome to the third edition of Neopoet Around The Globe, a collection celebrating the diverse voices and talents within our vibrant poetic community. This anthology showcases the achievements of our contest winners, whose exceptional work has resonated deeply with readers. We also recognize those who have fostered growth through their thoughtful and generous feedback, as well as the 'Neopoet Gems' selected by our contest department, each representing a unique spark within our community.

This edition is a testament to the dedication of our volunteers, from advocates to cabinet members, who work tirelessly to make Neopoet a welcoming and inspiring home for poets worldwide. As you delve into these pages, we hope you find inspiration, connection, and a renewed appreciation for the power of poetry. We eagerly invite those seeking a supportive community to join us and share their poetic journey.

~Trustees~

Milestones

Congratulations to the following members for reaching 5,000 or 10,000 comments on other members poetry.

10,000 Comments:

- Scribbler
- Geezer

5,000 Comments:

- Candlewitch
- Rula

Winners From Contest Entries 2024

I Lost The Instructions to being a woman

C.M. Mattison (Candlewitch)
Wisconsin, United States

I Lost The Instructions
to being a woman

You beat "Her" out of me
leaving my soul tattered.
In the beginning you were kind
warm and jovial, it mattered.

Gradually you began to change
taking me away from all I knew,
from Minnesota to the east coast
an easy ride we drove straight through.

I discovered your evil temper
on our trip, it left me in fear,
knocking me down, kicking me
you bellowed, shouting, making it clear.

You were the boss, and me your slave
seeing the cruel glint in your eye
was an omen of what was soon to come
you would test me in ways to make me cry...

Each new day was a promise of terror
you invented head-games to play.
In fear, I trembled trying to hide
tried not to anticipate the rue of the day.

Nights were bad too, I cowered under covers
You brutalized me sexually to hear me scream
threatening to blow my head off my shoulders
losing connection with my idea of a woman's dream!

The Wrathful sea

Ashley Sarath (Jokerface82)
Liverpool, United Kingdom

Her salted bludgeoning maw
swallowed vessels and galleys
with its green saline gullet of
ulcers
barnacles, and a throat full of oily
spots of acne sticky limpets

Treasures guarded by a circle
of sharks in an ocean restaurant
pinching crabs,
and swaying seaweed keeping naval
secrets.

A wave of wrathfulness, tossing
clubbing, floating ships, drowning
them into the abyss.
stripping seamen Into
skeletons with silent screams.

Supported by a howling killer
of a storm . Ripping, blowing holes
into arthritis wooden decks into oblivion
into the coldest dark depths.

World of the Living Dead

Karen Burns (Tigger Kaz)
Coventry, United Kingdom

A distant cackle of a witch
Spells a crafted costume, stitch by stitch.
Clanking bones are moving in the wind,
Jack skeleton winked before he grinned.

Pumpkin heads seem like they're alive,
Glinting in the moonlit drive.
Ghosts and ghouls came out to play,
On this Halloween scary day.

The corpse bride, with her shriveled head,
A scary beauty before she wed.
Sparking an image of fear or dread,
In this world of the living dead.

Grandious majestic mountain

Ashley Sarath (Jokerface82)
Liverpool, United Kingdom

There stood a majestic
Craggy face with razor blade
Edges of a monstrous
time honoured mountain

Turning its rocky nose up
at anything below him, robust
Jagged and risky, high stabbing
armour with White shark tip
Cut throated fins.

Bald rugged with a silent manner
cold stone as white as marshmallow
steep and strong, bold and old
broad frosted shoulders

With powdered freckles and a storm grey
complexion it wore a white necklace
and a frosted crown, made
by heaven.

Dreary day, long ride

Guy Caswell (Geezer)
New York, United States

Dreary day, on the thruway.
Sitting in Auntie Jean's '66 Bronze Barracuda fast-back,
radio plays softly, pop-Christmas stuff.
Long silence to a retreat for me; long drive.

Speaking out of the side of her face, [she had a way of that.]
She asked, "Are you so very sad that you lost the sight of your eye?"
Briefly, I saw that "Caswell" trait that she shared with my father.
A clearest blue, steadiest steel, and you knew that you would get the truth of whatever you heard. We all have it; the eye. Must be that Romney-gypsy blood.
"Yes, I am but more than that, I am glad that I still have one good eye to see the world. Even the bleak, grey day full of rain on the thruway.

The Proudest Moment

Hanh Chau (Hon)
California, United States

Far above I stand there
across from the blue sky
display as the great mountain
built with a strenuous height
of sturdy and mighty
portray as a strong image
raising to the deep climbing steps
through perseverance
with each challenge
When it comes to facing disaster
carrying with its strength
to conquer the fear of falling
continue to rise to the top
of the summit peak
achieving its goal as a champion
like a prize bringing home
with a jubilant feeling
of a great victory celebration

Feelings Lost

Clentin Martin (Clentin)
Pennsylvania, United States

We once embraced and knocked our knees
Now we are tied to our phones and keys

Human interaction seems to fade away
As our internet capabilities are here to stay

Plucking away on the facebook page
Sends me into an inner rage

Watching our young and how they react
Has changed our lives and that's a fact

How can we teach them how to enjoy a touch
A warm embrace, the thrill of a crush

Interaction is what we really need
To form a society that will be freed

To stop our moans and groans
We need to limit time on our phones!

Poetic Creations

Mark Loiselle (Mark)
Massachusetts, United States

It takes so long to let her live,
From way down deep, of herself, she shall give.
Innocent, unaware, helped with most care.
My love or my hell, to be done so well.

For weeks I sat and thought of her.
The words I write for her do say,
My love through night and through the day,
You surely live a lonely way.

Doubt and re-doubt.
Each line a part sought,
Each word carefully brought.
Thought and re-thought,
Taken to a whole,
Remains part of my soul.

Recipe for Love

Emma Gagnon (Hippiemoon)
Maine, United States

Pat-a-cake, pat-a-cake, baker's man
Find me a lover fast as you can
Find me a sweet boy, make it quick
Not too fast or I'll get sick.

Sick with love,
No cure by medicine.
Do you love me?
Don't be hesitant.

Hesitant love is not for me
Love me deep and true and free.
Do these things and you'll be mine
Be my boy til the end of time.

My First Internet Memory

Hanh Chau (Hon)
California, United States

My first internet memory
this brings me to the
introduction of the
tutorial study through
the google online
surfing with the
fascinating of
opportunity to acquire
for a learning desire in
a science technology
of today's global world
This interest starts from the
online searching to discover
unlimited learning ability tools
like an encyclopedia collection
with the resource information
for one share a broad
knowledge of understanding
through the adventure of
Internet Explorer with many
interesting selecting topics

Count and share your blessings

Karen Burns (Tigger Kaz)
Coventry, United Kingdom

The pace of life seems crazy,
In who it leaves behind.
Yet the greed of the wealthy,
Means too many do not mind.

A cavernous void, for the supposed lazy,
With few hands to lift them out.
When alright jacks have plenty,
Caring little for those with nought.

Empathy lacking, apethetic souls,
Blinded by selfish greed,
Have lost the ability,
To share with those in need

Narratives of competition,
Knocked their kindness away.
Changed their life's direction,
And led them all astray

Be not like these unkindly people,
Proffer a hand to help the poor.

For tomorrow is not yet come,
And you don't know what's in store.

Life changes on a hairpin,
your luck could turn around.
Fame and fortune today,
Tomorrow could run you aground.

Feel grateful for your blessings,
Leave jealousy at the door,
Share good fortune with each other,
And stop perpetually wanting more.

Mosquitos Suck

Willian Lynn (Willian Lynn)
Idaho, United States

Of all the creatures great and small
The one that I detest the very most,
The blood thirsty, damned mosquito,
I have no desire to be its dinner host.

The mosquito plays no favorites
It's most willing to drill and bite,
Everyone it darn well chooses,
There's no chance to wage a fight.

But fight I will with all I have
Be it sprays or creams or such,
I'll wear light colored clothing
But it doesn't help that much.

The pond down by the mill creek
Cricket sing their evening song,
A place where people love to fish
Until the mosquitoes come along.

A perfect campsite near the placid lake
Quiet ripples lace the still blue waters,
These times with family almost perfect
Until mosquitoes invade like squatters.

The fans on many Friday evenings
Sit in bleachers and the stands,
To watch their favorite teams at play
Until the mosquito squadron lands.

This critter has little earthly value
Not much to offer anyone,
It finds an unsuspecting target
Then dives and begins its evil fun.

These rotten little creatures lurk,
Only God knows why he made 'em,
I suppose that God already knows
How very much I truly hate 'em.

A Girl Named Indigo

Walter Rivas (Wallyroo92)
California, United States

They say she descended after one summer storm
Like a pretty reverie arched right out of the blue
With eyes so expressive as if they whispered secrets
That men were entranced by that delightful hue

Some say she emerged from the sea late after dusk
A balance of dark and light that nature surely dyes
Designed and crafted by the hand of a divine being
Because the ocean depths were captured in her eyes

Others will tell you she rose from a field of flowers
As if the flora had tinted her windows to the soul
Bearing a delicate semblance of love and mystery
Like art captivating hearts so beautiful and bold

But...

It was I who witnessed her sliding down a rainbow
On a spectrum of imagination where fantasies go
In a stream somewhere between violet and blue
In a winged surreal dream of a girl named Indigo

Ghostly Graveyard Warning

Paul Ray (Paleoray)
North Carolina, United States

When the pumpkins turn orange and maples turn red –
When the full moon is yellow and huge overhead;
When October night winds bring a chill to the air –
Never walk in a graveyard at midnight - Beware!

When the crickets stop chirping and bats screech and fly –
When a black cat appears in the wink of an eye;
When the trees look like figures that both point and stare –
Then avoid every churchyard at midnight - Beware!

For if you see these signs and you still pass that gate,
Then you've dug your own grave and you've sealed your own fate;
It's because in sepulchers there are ghosts with the power
To arise from the dead in that bewitching hour.

They are ruthless and restless sending chills as they moan,
And will scare you to pieces as they walk through each stone;
They will float over graves, they will fade, then appear –
Then the next thing you know they will wail in your ear.

You will scream and be frightened as long as you stay
In that special ground haunting and don't run away;

For the one hope you have that will set yourself free
Is to get both feet out of that cemetery!

So the next time you hear a bat screech in the night,
With an October moon that is yellow and bright;
And you pass by near midnight a grave while trees stare –
Then I say it once more to remind you - Beware!

Orchard of Choices

Shantelle Moyo (Shantelle Moyo)
Johannesburg, South Africa

In the orchard of choices, where branches extend,
Each apple a decision, a path without end.
Some gleam like the morning, tempting and bright,
While others hang heavy, shrouded in night.

With fingers outstretched, I wander the rows,
Sifting through options, where uncertainty grows.
A crisp red allure, promising sweet taste,
Yet caution whispers, "Don't rush; don't waste."

Beneath the green canopy, shadows entwine,
The weight of each choice, a burden divine.
Do I reach for the fruit that glistens with pride,
Or pause at the ones that humility hide?

Some apples are flawless, their surface a dream,
But inside they're hollow, or bursting at the seam.
Others, though bruised, hold a wisdom untold,
Lessons wrapped gently in skins worn and old.

With each chosen apple, a path starts to form,
A journey unfolding, both chaotic and warm.
For life is an orchard, vast and unplanned,
Where choices like fruits are plucked from the hand.

So I gather my harvest, both bitter and sweet,
Embracing the journey, no matter the feat.
In the orchard of choices, I learn to believe,
That each fruit has its story, and I am the weave.

In ripened reflection, I stand here today,
Grateful for moments that led me this way.
For every decision has brought me to see,
The beauty in choices, and the power in me.

Fear less

Karen Burns (Tigger Kaz)
Coventry, United Kingdom

Ribbons and buttons,
A haberdashery smile,
Perfectly crafted, by a long mile.
Practical decorations, well packaged placements.
Hidden within the depth of our basement.

All manner of scraps,
And material pieces.
All folded neatly, without any creases.
A plethora of memories, wrapped up into one,
From a bygone era that's long gone.

And at the same time,
Just as these flashbacks appear.
I hear a noise that fills me with fear.
A scratch then a squeak, I cannot find,
What cretins lurk to blow my mind?

A little searching,
Revealed a pair of twitching faces,
I'm ready to flee, as my heartbeat races.
But then I stop, and reconsider my fear,
As I wipe away a lone straying tear.

No more afraid of what lurks beneath,
In the darkest depths under there.
They've no more places to hide anywhere.
All horrors uncovered in a blink of an eye,
Illuminated by a crack portal to the sky.

With no more reasons to take flight,
I marvel at all that time forgot.
All the hidden gems not liked alot.
And as it all swirled around my mind,
I wondered why I left them behind.

My youthful days,
Not so much a haunting curse.
More a drumming rhythm and verse.
This happy place, brings back my smile,
The briefest comfort, by a long mile.

And as I stare at these forgotten gems,
Covered in dust and waiting to be found.
In their tomb capsules underground.
I make a pact to revisit my past,
To reveal the part of me I'd masked.

There's Always Tomorrow

Guy Caswell (Geezer)
New York, United States

I miss you, I miss the feel of your skin;
your cold hands as they seek the warmth of my neck.
I miss the smell of your breath, Pepsi, cigarettes, and love.
The chuckles of amusement at the tickle of chill fingers.
Holding on to each other until we are warm, and the day takes us away.

Today, you go about the business of static living, unforgiving.
You don't know me, I can't forget, you won't remember.
Roommates with history, lovers before doubt.
Is it you? Is it me? Who wins?
Head games require more effort

Tomorrow I will try harder.
I have enough noises in my head this morning.
Today I will coast, stay loose, let it be.
Tomorrow, I will be rested, retuned and sharper, maybe a winner...
Yeah, tomorrow should be a good day.

At the X-Mas Bar

Guy Caswell (Geezer)
New York, United States

As I passed by the sitting booth
in the X-Mas bar and grill,
I saw Mr. and Mrs. Santa
sit down to have a swill.

He patted her on the bum,
she kissed him on the cheek,
I distinctly heard her say,
Boy, what a wretched week!

He said; Yeah, I know it hon,
but it's all over now.
We had some terrifying moments,
but we got through somehow.

We had to can elf Albert,
he ate my stash of magic cookies.
He tried to hit on you, my love,
looking for some nookie.

Then the reindeer went on strike,
wanting fresher hay and feed,
and Rudolph, with that damned nose
got them all to smoking weed!"

Well, get us another drink my dear,
I'll rack the table for a game of pool.
Then off to bed at the North Pole,
where you can make love to this old fool.

Waking Up Naked

Clentin Martin (Clentin)
Pennsylvania, United States

Waking up Naked
Seeing the bright light above
Sends fear to my heart

Cancelled

Ashley Sarath (Jokerface82)
Liverpool, United Kingdom

Slate grey stretched skies
winding snake, skidding sloshing
roads, cold choking cloaks of
icey hugs and screaming wind
tugs. Falling flake feathers
pale as cocaine

Bobble hat wearing brats
lobbing frosty white
spheres, causing stripes
of creamed powdered
crowned cars, to smack

and crash, under a,
concealment of falling
white rain. Brandberry

red faces and blushing
noses, infuriating drivers,
doors flying open with
shaking raging fists

catapulting angry words
at mobs of yob minded

brats. Now Christmas
Eve is mad, packed its
sacked, it's, been hijacked
by mitten gloved douchebags.

The Downward Spiral

Sancha Glasgow-Regis (Merlicka)
New Jersey, United States

Incoherent chatter
24 pack almost done
Staring blankly at the dawn
Another bottle in his hand

Such a beautiful life diminished
Lost hope, great despair
A slow descent through darkness,
Sadly commenced by
Just one beer.

One beer turned into many
Like a fountain, watch them flow
Rushing down like a torrent
His count, he doesn't know

Life's now a drag, no more ambition
He ponders defeatedly "how did i get here?"
Sadly realizing it started with the decision
Of having
just one beer

Lovergirl

Emma Gagnon (Hippiemoon)
Maine, United States

I'll be your perfect little lovergirl
Writing you poems
And singing you songs

I'll be your perfect little lovergirl
Whatever you say goes,
You can do no wrong.

I'll be your perfect little lovergirl
Don't worry about me,
I'm always fine.

I'll be your perfect little lovergirl
Get high off your kiss
Get drunk off cheap wine.

I'll be your perfect little lovergirl
Play with my heart,
It's yours to abuse.

I'll be your perfect little lovergirl
Go with other girls
It's me you can use.

I'll be your perfect little lovergirl
You'll think I'm fucking crazy
And maybe you're right.

I'll be your perfect little lovergirl
My emotions change quickly
Like day into night.

I'll be your perfect little lovergirl
You'll knock me right down
But I'll stay by your side.

I'll be your perfect little lovergirl
Make me feel how you want
The tears always subside.

I'll be your perfect little lovergirl
Like a loyal old dog
I won't give up on you.

I'll be your perfect little lovergirl
I'll stay by your side
Til I'm sure that we're through.

Steven

C.M. Mattison (Candlewitch)
Wisconsin, United States

Ten years, I went with a sealed heart
living with the rules I had self-imposed.
Do not get too close or let "Him" in,
love is no option! This window is closed!

On my own having taken good care
not get mixed-up with yet another man.
Years in school, an associates degree
next, the Air Force and travel was my plan!

Having just met, I told of my goal
all through the night you worked to change my mind.
Through the day you convinced me to stay
for you could see that I was flying blind .

I stuck around, to learn about you ,
kindness in your smile and your quiet ways
talking and listening to each other
striking a chord, binds the rest of our days.

I had a rudder but I was a ship with no mast,
I found my superhero at last !

Hope

Anna Severchuk (Anna Severchuk)
Odessa, Ukraine

Somewhere along the way, the system was broken,
Leaving hearts cold, and dreams unspoken.
Yet, in the darkness, a whisper starts,
A flicker of hope, that warms our hearts.
For though the path ahead seems bleak and dire,
There's still a spark, a flickering fire.

We hope you can still hear us, God,
Because humanity is lost, in a sea of mud.
The air grew thick with sorrow's sting,
A broken song, the echoes cling.
We search for light, in the shadows deep,
And vow to mend the wounds we keep.
For beauty still exists, though hidden now,
And hope for a better tomorrow, somehow.

Trials and Triumphs

Shelby Pryor (Shelby Pryor)
Tennessee, United States

At Midnight tonight
As the clock clicks
Its another birthday
Another age shifts

It's been a hard year
Not ideal at best
The triumphs make
It worth the test

On a cold, snowy night
My life had only begun
Seventeen years have passed
Yet I'm nowhere near done

So here's to a year full of
Success and desires awoke
To a new year of happiness
To another barrier broke

A year is a measure of time
Only created in the mind
I wonder what would happen
If to time we were blind

So goodbye, sweet sixteen
You taught me many a lesson
I wouldn't change a thing
When all is said and done

Hello, seventeen years old
And to all the unseen bumps
I'll try to make you proud
Through the trials and triumphs

From the Wilows

Mark Loiselle (Mark)
Massachusetts, United States

We gazed at the psychedelic sun
blazing an undefined path on melting asphalt
the soles of our naked feet could not feel
as our pinwheel hillsides had become barren
except for the fireworks of memories
or the beauty of our youth.

Mummified angels with blood stained wings
we could not see what was real.

Your living turned dragon black
as you shared the poison that became our good-byes.
You could only hear,
and not speak back to the love
that had followed you all along.

Your own flesh would not leave your side
crying sympathy
for what you once were ...

a colorful young garden.

Insights of an orphan

Lorraine Peterson (lostLA)
Kentucky, United States

in no will I am named
To a birthright I have no claim
I rummage through the lives of man
Foraging from them what I can
Right from wrong it's hard to tell
For I'm still holding the keys to hell

Call me guilty, I am not
Lock me up until I rot
You've viewed the past & still can't see
Call me guilty & I shall be

The thread of life that keeps us sane
Is beginning to show signs of strain
Triggers released within our minds
Creating stutters & empty time

Call me guilty, I am not
Lock me up until I rot
Line your pockets with filthy change
Allowing the guilty to be free of chains

Not a dime, have I left to pay
For all my wealth was stole away

But in the end, the good book speaks
We only sow what we can reap

Call me guilty, I am not
Lock me up until I rot
If reality is what I perceive
Does yours differ from what I see?

Overdraft the Monster

Guy Caswell (Geezer)
New York, United States

As the wind howls, I am reminded...
Reminded of the rippling sheet of rain,
a silver curtain billowing across the roof.
There will be water in the attic.

There is an overdraft there, going over.
The spirit of the storm, travels so fast,
it carries water over the edge, to the window below;
dropped, it clings to the wall, and sneaks in.

I've known about that overdraft, for quite some time.
I watched it as a child, awakened by the wind.
The monster that ate at my home, needed company,
I heard the pitiful moans, as the spirit tore at the shingles.

Now, we are together again, the spirit and I;
I am tempted to join it as it drags its familiar water
over the edge and into the draft, but no!
I cannot cling to the wall and re enter the house.

That would be an overdraft that I could not afford.

Bogeyman

Carrie Chovan (RoseBlack)
New York, United States

Eyes glowing red, he lives not under your bed,
the taunting voice within your head.
A shadow of a man haunting your dreams,
twisting reality until it isn't what it seems.

He's around every corner, lying in wait.
Every breath he breathes, filled with hate.
The demon is alive and on the streets,
disguised as a worthy lover between the sheets.

And once he has you in his grasp,
the pain and torture will make you gasp.
There's no way out, no matter how loud you shout.
Love isn't what the bogeyman is about.

Abandoned

Mary Beth Magee (Mary Beth Magee)
Mississippi, United States

She bobbed there in the gentle swell,
The little boat I knew so well.
The sail wrapped tight along the boom
Gave me a feeling of dark doom.
I saw no anchor chain hung down
To stop her, lest she run aground.
No one sat in her empty bow.
No hand controlled her keel just now.
A gentle breeze set her to rock.
How did she get loose from the dock?
As the breeze caused her to turn,
I spotted paint along her stern.
Rough letters where my name had been -
The words now looked like "Mortal Sin."
What had he done in dark of night?
Was he convicted by dawn's light?
Then in the reeds beside the dock...
What I saw gave me quite a shock.
A body, face down, on the lake,
Could it be him, for heaven's sake?
Please, no, I prayed and backed away.
What pushed him so, I cannot say.
I didn't dream that he would dare.
I only know I lost him there.

Bon Fire

Carrie Chovan (RoseBlack)
New York, United States

Moon high; middle of the night.
Drums thumping; bumping in hypnotic flight.
Cloaked hoods fall to the ground,
scattered chants mix with the eerie sound.

Candle wax burns at the fingertips;
Hecate's breath embraces swaying hips.
Shadows dance amongst the flames,
linking spirits to our world without shame.

'Tis our season, witches take hold,
The magic runs hot and bold.
Our veil is thinning, hear the roar of the thunder,
when the living and the dead are no longer asunder.

A Bard's Bad Luck

Michael Keens (Michael Keens)
Hampshire, United Kingdom

Sing to me Muse, of a day of your choosing
I hope it's not rude, but somewhat amusing
We've all travelled far and await in suspense
As your bard I now ask, please commence.

The day was short but the sun still hot
A sundial displayed it was one o'clock
What happened that day was enough to shock
An Athenian man stole a cow and time stopped.

Helios' rage on that short summer's day
Had him fuming and musing over who should then pay
I alone know the culprit and surely, I'll say
He is a giant in size with a scar on his face.

The scar in question is the shape of a bull
Six inches wide and not equally tall
It's said he's gifted with words and tells stories to all
And rarely goes hungry so is usually full.

Well, it may seem that my Muse is a rat
I have that scar on my face and I'm more than quite fat
Yes, I travel and talk and write as I walk
But muses can lie through their teeth, with eyes of a hawk.

Evil Tinker Toys

C.M. Mattison (Candlewitch)
Wisconsin, United States

Tinker and twiddle
in this workshop of mine,
always examining
the toys witch I find.

Fixing the broken
mini pianos and doll,
the sailboats, kites
and balls where they fall.

There are other
things that I find,
when I go out walking
after I've dined.

souls where I find them
all tattered and torn,
the promising faithless
battle-scared and forlorn.

Drowning in the gutter,
down on ragged knees
making promises sweet,
all ready to please.

Ripe with excuses
all of them lame,
professing to come clean
in this ancient game.

Men, mostly women
redemption, not wanting,
pleading to be spared
from the memories haunting.

I see their true selves,
horrendous deeds done.
In the lie of loving,
bullets fired for fun.

Back at my workshop
I'll take them apart...
Like wet tinker toys,
kidney liver and heart!

Who Am I, Even?

Paula Frew (Punkyfrewster)
Ohio, United States

I look in my
purse, and my
wallet is missing.

I sit down to
give it a more
thorough look.

The wallet is lost.
An existential
crisis arises.

No license.
No pictures.
No credit cards.

I grapple with
who I am
and if I am.

Terrors of the Young

Ian Frank Rolf (Alex Tanner)
Isle Of Wight, United Kingdom

In darkness he lies
Blankets up to his chin,
Eyes stare into blackness
Would the monsters rush in?

Tap tap on the window,
Scritch scratch, rustle rustle;
Just a branch from a tree
Scrapes the pane, tenses muscle.

From its hide behind clouds
A bright moon appears,
Casts shadows on curtains
To build up his fears.

Nerves stretch as a fiddle
Taut for the bow,
Buries deeper 'neath blankets
Whimpers loud, fast and low.

He remembers the girl,
The terror that drove
Her on through the trees
As winds howled, boughs bowed.

Branches clawed out like talons
Her soft flesh to rend;
She screamed, ran and stumbled
As her life did depend.

Now the terror was his
The wind howled loud
From hell they were coming
Deep he trembled and cowed.

The door bursts wide open
Light floods coal black room
Dispelling the darkness
Saving him from doom:

"What is that shouting?"
His mother stands there
Hastened to see up
Steep wooden stairs:

"Nightmares again?
I'll say one last time,
No more watching Snow White
Before your bedtime".

Loving You

Emma Gagnon (Hippiemoon)
Maine, United States

Loving you is as beautiful as a sunset.
Running through empty art museums,
Laughing when we are out of breath.
It feels as infinite as the stars in the sky,
As certain as the sun rising another day.

Loving you is a lifeboat in a storm,
My most favorite pair of shoes,
A good book on a rainy day.

Let's pick petals off of flowers to verify our love.
Dance in parking lots in the light of your car,
Kiss me in the rain just like in the movies.

Cupid's struck us with his arrows,
And every day I fall more.
Hold me in your arms again,
And make our love a tale of folklore.

Broken Glass

C.M. Mattison (Candlewitch)
Wisconsin, United States

She was a dancer
on dark paved streets,
she had vibrations in her soul
always music in her head.

Could not keep still,
her bare feet ever
tapping out the rhythm
of a distant melody.

Each day saw changes
on her preferred stage,
trash cans overflow
garbage in the streets.

Alarmed, a child pointed out;
"Look, Mom she's bleeding!"
(they looked on in shock)
As she danced on broken glass.

Coal Mine Canary

Emma Gagnon (Hippiemoon)
Maine, United States

Do you know about coal mine canaries?
They used to take caged birds down into the coal mines,
And when they would die the workers would know to leave too.

Let me be a canary in your chest.
Let me live inside your rib cage,
Feel your heart beat for me,
Watch your blood flow through your veins.

Keep me safe next to your heart
And I'll keep you safe from all that's bad.

Use me as your compass,
I'll tell you to run when things get hard.

Let me be your coal mine canary.
Let me sacrifice myself to save you from the inevitable.

Whispering Woods

Howard Osborne (Twizzle48)
Yorkshire, United Kingdom

Perhaps the rustling leaves are telling the tree's tale
Whispering, such that only those listening may hear
Only when it is in tune, may the message be clear
Yet unless easily understood, it will be of little avail

The breeze is a medium, but other connections too
To share, an underground root network also serves
It's communication via a kind of complex of nerves
No myths or stories, as all that's shared will be true

Summer is a competition for sunlight, as if in a duel
In autumn it is time for the farewell to falling leaves
Yet the first snow of winter is as an axe that cleaves
But next spring, it's the buzz of growth and renewal

The style of the telling is not random, but planned
Facts the trees near and far, eventually get to know
But its sending and receipt is effective, even if slow
Nature's sagas few of us will ever get to understand

The Purge

Carrie Chovan (RoseBlack)
New York, United States

The siren blares,
one, two, three....
it's me, the last thing you'll see.
And sadly, no one cares.

Life put the gun in my hand,
a knife at my side,
with no where to hide,
before all is banned.

What was that you said?
Through stitched up lips,
bullet holes in your hips.
You'd rather be dead?.

Cool metal against your skin
betrayal is now a deadly sin,
punishing the offenders,
the great pretenders,

You'll never hurt anyone again.

Broken Air Condition

Kristen Hardigree (Kristen H.)
Georgia, United States

We never had much more than each other
in the summer of 2016

Adventures on Saturday nights
Two wheels
Two helmets
Two hearts

Lazy Sunday mornings
Two cups of coffee
Two cigarettes burned
Two hands together

There wasn't much to it
Just you and I,
and our broken air conditioner

2:23AM

Zachary Stabb (Zach)
Montreal, Canada

It's quiet, but my thoughts are alive
It's dark, but there are fireworks in my mind
It's still, but my soul rocks
It's calm, but the silence stops
It's peaceful, but something is abound
It's serene, but my ear hears a sound
A sound of someone I know
A sound of somewhere i've been
The smell of fresh air
The leaves in the wind
To a setting sun
Reminding me of your glow
From a coastal town
Forgotten long ago
The peace flows through me
And my body drifts to sleep
Goodnight my sweet
Let's dream tomorrow

In The Dark Night

John Leslie Boydstun (Leslie)
Utah, United States

In the dark night
shadows move swiftly.
Carrying burdens
greivous to be born.

Brandishing pitchforks
lanterns and axes.
Off on a witch hunt
to settle an incident.

Innocent victims
abused for their differences.
Knowing not why they'd been
driven from their homes.

On with the tyranny
there by the waters edge!
Silenced in terror
at the first light of dawn

Deprived and destitute
there in the morning.
Hung by the neck
to end the alarm.

Dancing In The Dark

Willian Lynn (Willian Lynn)
Idaho, United States

The candle burning on the mantle ledge
Flames dancing on this darkened night,
Remind me of the two of us in love
While we danced 'till morning's light.

The picture hanging in the hallway
Others neatly framed and on display,
Show us living life for all it's worth
I remember every fun filled day.

I wonder what went so wrong
Was it me or was it you?
I know there's blame to share
But I'll always wish I knew.

Our friends still ask about you
I would like to say "she's fine",
Truthfully I guess I'll never know,
I think about you all the time.

The lamp glowing by the window
I'll keep lit and hope you'll see,
Your picture, and know you're welcome,
And you'll come in and dance with me.

Locked In A Basement

Carrie Chovan (RoseBlack)
New York, United States

Behind concrete walls,
entombed by damp wood and mold,
even though he loved her more,
than any master should.

He gauged her eyes one at a time,
replacing them with glass beads,
while she writhed in pain.
An unwilling compromise.

Stitched up lips, needle and thread.
His secret kept, as she silently wept,
Blood soaked tears ran down her face,
how she wished she was dead.

Mounting her head on a stick,
he fixed her hair with a sigh.
Such a shame how she bled.
As he dragged her lifeless torso to bed.

Winter Cometh

Howard Osborne (Twizzle48)
Yorkshire, United Kingdom

Do you hear winter, I hear it coming
That distant growl, there in the wind
Stronger now, than an autumn breeze
With the merest hint of an early freeze
And with no sweet taste like tamarind
But a biting cold that can be numbing

For some, it is a season for celebration
But its hidden scowl suggests otherwise
Hearing threats under its frozen breath
Of ice and snow, laying so still in death
Pretty snowflakes offering cute disguise
As so much of Nature is in hibernation

At least this is true in Northern climes
Just bleak with not much give and take
And still, some try to understand why
As the end of the calendar year is nigh
But there is hope following in its wake
Anticipating the Spring's warmer times

The Shadow Knows

Dipak Sen (Sen99)
Nottingham, United Kingdom

Examine your shadow self
A darker side that lives in stealth
In unguarded moments it shows
What's hidden inside, only the Shadow knows

A dark clusters of thorns
That strangled the rose
Why it didn't survive
Only the shadow knows

Waging an internal war
When friends turn to foes
An ugly side reveals itself
Only the shadow knows

A fighter hawk descends on a dove
Why are you at war with what you love
There will be remorse after the abuse
Too weak to resist, there's just no use

What bothers and troubles
Don't try and ignore
Something concealed right at the core
Like a quiet cancer it grows, only the shadow knows

The blood turns black
And the anger grows
Your true self is trapped
Only the Shadow knows

Shadows get longer than the evening sun
How far can you run into the mouth of darkness ?

The Quill-Poet's Parley

Rula Younis Ali Hijazi (Rula)
Amman, Jordan

With a rustic nib, burnt out and done,
An undusted feather laid down, forlorn.
Whispering days an endless despair,
"Forsake me not in the attic's stale air."

"I had the aspiration, I had the will,
I always admired you, my precious quill.
You were my pal through tough times,
We often crafted some good rhymes."

What happened then? What went wrong?
Why did you neglect me that long?
Did you desert me for a better friend?
Could this be our friendship's end?

"Never shall I relinquish you

For we're one, never two

Revive my quill, let stories ignite

Together we'll conquer the glooms of night."

Shore Watch

Paul Ray (Paleoray)
North Carolina, United States

Splashing, crashing sound the waves
On the surf and then retrieve;
As the foam spreads on the sand,
While the pipers dash and weave.

High above the seagulls glide,
Circling 'round a sea of teal;
Others swooping close to pier,
Looking for an easy meal.

In the distance dolphins dive,
With their synchronizing breaks;
Dorsal fins shine at each peak,
Then they submerge in their wakes.

Sand crabs scurry back and forth,
Seeking food along the shore;
After catching fish with claws,
Quick they vanish as they bore.

Soon the sun sets in the west,
As the moon brings mirrored light;
Ocean tides smooth out the sand,
While the waves gleam through the night.

What My Best Friend Gave Me

Mark Loiselle (Mark)
Massachusetts, United States

My best friend gave me the truth, his age when I asked, thirty-two, in his dark brown leather jacket.
First and last time I ever asked that question, all dressed in white, sunny day of first communion.
Slight hesitation before he spilled the beans, knowing the truth couldn't hurt, and didn't.
Still have pictures from that day, a sunny day, back in the nineteen fifties, Saint Michaels Church.

My best friend gave me an education, My Fair Lady, when he realized that I had a little impediment.
Taught me the value of pronunciation, importance of being understood, by those who valued that.
The idea of confidence in myself, faced with others who were confident as well, held my head high.
The Rain in Spain, how to speak in song, it all seemed long, I had been wrong, and I got it.

Music, from Ma's pots and pans came a rhythm, a clamoring she didn't mind, the kitchen floor.
My best friend, and the Polka Dots, big band, big drums, then I knew, knew the real sound.

Gave me exposure to all the right things, from all the right places, people.

My best friend gave me rope, fifty feet of half inch, "I want to climb" and so I did.
Gave me the tools, set me free, on my own, I turned into me!

My best friend, my dad, I miss him so much, in the end, I am just like him.

The Last Time

Mary Beth Magee (Mary Beth Magee)
Mississippi, United States

I've spent my life waiting in line.
Sometimes first, sometimes last,
Sometimes in the middle,
By age or by height, steadfast
I stood, sometimes by school grade
But in all those times past
Someone else set the order.
Down the hall or before the mast,
I was told where to stand.
But this time I'm ready to go past
The others in line. This time, to me
Alone the line to the next phase is cast.
I shall leave the line behind
And step through to eternity vast.

The Visitor

Mary Beth Magee (Mary Beth Magee)
Mississippi, United States

You visit for a moment,
Accept a breath of hospitality,
Then dash away again.
You share your company briefly.

But in that time, oh,
The magic you bring.
From tiny eggs to instars
To gloriously patterned wing.

I watched you hatch and crawl,
Grow, shed and wriggle.
You change your dress. Your
New look makes me giggle.

You give me joy and delight
With your aerial ballet.
My royal friend, magician,
Harlequin at play,

Dear monarch, share your gift
Of grand, exuberant joy
With all. Give us eyes to
See, and feelings to employ.

You set an example
Of living in the moment.
Let us live so our days
Are likewise spent.

Dash on, my friend,
Your destiny calls.
Send your children my way
When the milkweed grows tall.

Spring Fling

Caroline Joy Hateley (Carrie)
Perth, Australia

You came into the world,
In September, it was Spring!
Unplanned, yet full of life,
A tiny little thing.

Your smile was like the sun,
You lit up a darkened room
Your eyes reflected who you were
You grew up, far too soon.

The love you have, inside of you,
Your heart could be, the flower.
Standing brightly in your garden
Your stems, they give you power.

So here you are in this Spring fling,
For all of us to see.
In full bloom, that small wee thing,
Was really just old me.

Along The Windy Shore

Diane Pryor (Lavender)
Indiana, United States

I remember you
and your lit-up smile
under the salty boardwalk.
You were seventeen
with your tousled hair
along the windy shore.

Such a time we had
'neath the summer sun
under the salty boardwalk.
With our hands entwined
we would race the waves
along the windy shore.

We never made promises
we couldn't keep.
No promises were broken.

So in the silver moonlight
there on the beach,
few words were ever spoken.

I remember soon
summer days grew short

under the salty boardwalk.
I was seventeen
when we said goodbye
along the windy shore.

Do you remember me
with my deep brown eyes
under the salty boardwalk?
Part of me remains
racing with the waves
along the windy shore.

I'm there along the shore.

'59 Plymouth

Guy Caswell (Geezer)
New York, United States

For sale: 1959 Plymouth 4-dr. Blk. with red interior.
318 V-8, with 4bbl. auto-transmission
65, 000 mi. needs new battery and tune-up
Clear title, no liens - $65.00 firm.

It was love at first sight,
long, dark and intriguing
just a little bit rusted,
she said, to me screaming,

"Take me home sweetheart
You won't be sorry"
I forked over the loot,
my eyes were all starry.

A scrub and a tune-up
new battery 'n more
derusted and painted
mended holes in the floor

I learned all her tricks
we went everywhere
We had many adventures
and I've stories to share

We parted at last,
too tired was she
I traveled long distance
I set her free...

To a little old lady,
I gave her away
They both went to heaven
the very next day.

Old blinded eyes,
in the sun's setting glare
couldn't see the new sign
the Bridge Out, Beware

An untimely demise
for both, I'm afraid
The '59 Plymouth
and the little old maid.

Chase

Manja Stojanovic (Mini)
Nis, Serbia

On the road where dreams unfold,
Adventure calls with stories untold.
Wheels turning to freedom's call,
Guided by a beckoning drawl.

Ahead lies a vast expanse,
Leaving behind the past's dance.
Sunsets paint the evening sky,
As stars twinkle up on high.

From dusty paths to city streets,
Nature's beauty, where the beauty meets
Faces met along the way,
Each one adding to our day.

Mountains high, valleys low,
Time's passing, memories grow.
Through the unknown we make our way,
On this journey, come what may.

Whispers of the wind, tears of the sky,
Moments fleeting as days fly by.
Endless roads, twists and turns,
On this journey, our hearts yearn.

Footsteps marking time and space,
Seeking a never-ending chase.
Every mile, a part of our whole,
On the road, finding our soul.

This Is Our Golden Hour, My Love

Kristen Hardigree (Kristen H.)
Georgia, United States

Maybe in the next life
we'll be birds...
free as the breeze,
watching the golden hour
from our favorite tree,
snuggling close in the winter months
in our nest made from the bones
of this lifetime

The Unwanted Kiss

C.M. Mattison (Candlewitch)
Wisconsin, United States

2714 Girard Ave. N. Ghost Tales #3
The Unwanted Kiss

Sour lips pressed to mine in the night
breath the like of which to peel paint !
Push hard against the weight on my chest
harder still, I'm ready to faint

How can a ghost exert such willing
dominance over the living ?
Sitting up sharply I catch my wind
He's taking what I'm not 'giving'

Severely stressed over this, I'm wrecked
not sleeping well numerous nights,
my brain will not shut down long enough...
I must stay near the brightest lights!

When I close my eyes, I see His face
wide red eyes staring into mine
Nerves on fire, I manage to get up
to the bathroom... here, but not fine!

More mad than frightened, splashing my face,
seeing my image in the glass

hot tears of rage welling up to flow...
incredulous! How can this pass?

It's three a.m. I'm up for the day.
Who could sleep after what I found?
Under the covers, I dress myself,
feeling His presence all around

Some one older, wiser than myself,
might know better what's to be done
Who can I turn to with this problem?
not my idea of good fun...

I am only fourteen for Christ's sake!

Come One, Come All

Nora VanDerMeid (MermaidMaster)
New York, United States

What is Love if not fucking crazy,
What is love if not burning desire,
throwing yourself off a cliff,
red-hot steam rising from the fire.

Give me a love that is real, that is brutal,
that'll tear me apart at the seams.
I want it to be the stuff of fantasies,
fulfill every desire, satiate every dream.

Let love tempt me with her serpentine ways,
I will take the biggest, sweetest bite.
I'll brush the salt lines off my windowsill,
and unlock my doors, an open invite.

"Come one, Come all, One night only,
Come and gaze as a crazed girl burns"
What is love if not a goddamned circus,
A spectacle made to be dazzling and adored.

I'll race down highways and tear through small towns,
I'll go wherever Love wants to take me.
Lace up my boots, and never turn around
For what is love if not fucking crazy?

Something New

Shelby Pryor (Shelby Pryor)
Tennessee, United States

Rain rushes from the skies
Mixing with a single tear
The wind cuts through
Like every doubt, every fear

Lightning shatters my peace
Like the pieces of my mind
A distant thunderclap mocks
Of the girl I was and left behind

A tornado rages in my head
Demolishing my peace and joy
I plaster on a smile for you,
But it's just a tactic I employ

The fear paralyzes my heart
Yet I'm so tired of being afraid
It is time to get up and fight
Before my resolve starts to fade

My fingers curl around my sword
I lift it high, I've got my armor on
I bring it down with all my strength
Until the shattered pieces are gone

There is no fixing the girl I was
No use in buying time with glue
The only solution is to shatter her
And forge with fire Something New

The Naughtiest Naughty of All

Diane Pryor (Lavender)
Indiana, United States

You know Harry and Marv
The Joker and Brutus
Darth Vader and Sauron
The Grinch who'd "de-Who" us.

Hannibal Lecter
Cruella De Vil
Honed Freddy Krueger
Cute Gremlins who kill.

Bug-filled Oogie Boogie
Wicked Witch and her broom
Ebenezer Scrooge
In his thrice-haunted room.

Michael Corleone
Godfather, ill-famed
The Dark Lord of Hogwarts
"He-Who-Must-Not-Be-Named."

But do you recall
The Naughtiest Villain of all?

(Da-da, dum-dum)

That little creepy shelf elf
Hiding there above my head
Eavesdropping on my every word
Ratting to The Man In Red.

He and his flimsy arms and legs
Resting near the fireplace
I wanna fling him to the flames
Watch his brown-nosed, blazing face.

Elf on the Shelf is such a fink
Tattling on my every whim
I'd like to toss him in the creek
Dank, and wet, and very dim.

Then one night, I'd had enough
Of goody-two-shoes' snitches
Yanked that elf right off the shelf
And ripped open all his stitches.

Now I'm a happy caroler
I can be my naughty self
Singing this version of "Rudolph"
Finishin' off that freaky elf.

Dear, dad

Siphosethu Thobela (Angie S)
Gauteng, South Africa

I want to thank you for all the empty promises,
for the hot air full of birthday wishes.
Living vicariously through daddy-daughter dates
how I wondered how it felt to be daddy's princess,
to be the apple of your eye: your first concern and interest
is something I desperately yearned for.

I want to thank you for giving mom love
with your violent, fistful hug.
Where I saw smiles, you gave indifferent shrugs.
Where I saw kindness and affection, you gave dishonesty and mistrust.
If speaking was a form of communication, silence was echoed in our house.
We were different from others.

Primary school was my solace,
I kept away from boys; trauma is a dark place.
'Fake it till you make it', I put on my happy face.
Reading was my favourite escape.
The screeching arguing, that always escalated.
I matured before my prime, my childish state eaten.

High school was my slow internal detonation.
A withering flower, I was nearing self-destruction.
We spoke less and less, there was no connection.

I slept more and more, drowning in depression.
Self-loathing, I fed myself to a slice of masochism,
telling myself I'd never become a victim.

You've taught me independence and resilience,
Like a Hitler recruit I fought with resistance
not to be filled with hate, anger and impatience.
I can see unrequited love with no compassion.
And when I do, it's to you I give salutation.

Thank you, dad.

Ways of loving

Marie-Amelie Floquet (Terumi Sakurai)
La Ciotat, France

Wonder of the world
And blessing for my heart
You appeared in my life like a
Shining star on my path

Only you, only your love
Forever in my heart

Longing for you, eternally
On the road to your heart; I'm
Venturing, hesitantly
Infinitely stuck in me; I'll
Never let you go, as you're a
Gift for my soul that's making it shine.

Of The Night

Diane Pryor (Lavender)
Indiana, United States

Where is the
Great Gray Owl
hiding
from north winds
and winter
snows?

In his home
above Earth
abiding -
only the
wise, full moon
knows.

Where are the
stellar lights
shining
when self-willed
clouds do not
appease?

In his home
above Earth
pining -

only the
wise, full moon
sees.

Who are the
lonely souls
crying
when night falls
over lands
below?

In his home
above Earth
sighing -
only the
wise, full moon
may know.

What of the
owls, the stars,
and kin
when needing
radiance
within?

Above Earth
in his home
divine,

the wise, full
moon will bow,
then shine.

To My Monarch and Her Milkweed

Diane Pryor (Lavender)
Indiana, United States

You begin so tiny, My Little One,
just a whisper of an egg on a Milkweed leaf.
But there you are, mellow, yellow, and striped,
delicate, yet somehow stoic
as you tenderly dream.

Soon pillar, pillar Caterpillar, off you go!
to eat, and eat the Milkweed leaf, its welcoming
home, almost yours alone, guarding and
protecting you with
its milky cream.

You shed your skin as you grow and grow,
bright orange, white, and black spiral around you,
stripes over stripes as your lovely
Milkweed offers its kindness
and sweetest esteem.

What happens next? It's so amazing, You Clever Gem!
You spin a base and hang below, spinning, spinning, spinning
from your loyal Milkweed as you both wait and wait,
anticipate, the miracle of life ever changing
in your small space.

Soon you sleep, My Dear, now beheld as a chrysalis,
a secure home as you dream about the fresh air, the sun,
the breeze flowing through your tender Milkweed flower,
its gentleness still holding you there,
keeping you in its grace.

I am overjoyed as your dreams unfold, unfold, unfold...

Oh, I have no words for what blooms and becomes --
it is YOU, glorious you, Lovely Butterfly! Now free
to flutter and fly, and fly and flutter amid your Milkweed friend
in the fresh air, the sun, and the wind --
it's all yours to embrace.

Your Milkweed keeps you in its care,
your every need lingering there.
And when you leave, as you shall do,
its love and devotion will go with you.

I admire you as you flutter by,
My Dearest, Darling Butterfly.
Your colors, bold! Your wings remark
of your joy and zeal as a new Monarch.

My Pal Jet

Ian Frank Rolf (Alex Tanner)
Isle Of Wight, United Kingdom

I named him Jet.
My favourite pet,
The only pet I ever owned,
Dad found him wandering in a field,
Picked him up and brought him home;
We were friend and playmates for
Oh! I don't know how long
Till the day he decided to leave;
One morning he was there, by evening, gone,
No clue as to where he may be;
I hunted for days, in hedgerows and fields
but I never saw him again;
I hope he was happy, maybe found a mate
To sire more of the tortoise strain.

A Way Out

Rula Younis Ali Hijazi (Rula)
Amman, Jordan

As night pulls down its wild dark curtains
And heavy eyelids drop lazily,
I ponder with spider-like loomed shadows,
Thoughts torture my broken, weary soul.

Everything around my room plays tricks;
Shadows with shattered hearts wander,
Carrying bloody, slaughtered dreams,
All howl, moan in pain, "that's insane, that's insane."

I seek a way out, is there no escape?
The door's locked with heavy chains.
Windows, it seems, are all covered with tar,
Behind the sill, bars add weight.

Then more spirits seep in, multiplying,
From nowhere, to heighten the scene.
I try to cry, but my own voice chokes me,
Then a louder voice declares, "There is no way out."

Two seat bench

Stan Holliday (Scribbler)
South Carolina, United States

The treated wood on this deer stand
is fading grey from all the years
which matches these woods old and bland.
I check for rot as autumn nears
and last night's ground fog disappears.

Carefully I ascend the ladder
and it creaks like my brittle bones.
It holds me so it doesn't matter.
Through these deep woods the wind moans
with desultory low pitched tones.

I step from ladder onto rough cut blind;
it's almost level and nearly square
but I reckon the deer will not mind
as they pass from here to there
checking their range with intent stare.

It looks like the roof doesn't leak,
I shake the walls, the braces hold.
The openings will let me peek
come the months when winds blow cold.
My exam is not complete, all told.

I turn toward that I'd as soon not see
A bench which I once built for two
an old friend who used to hunt with me.
I knew not then his hunts were through.
Too many spots in where his doom grew.

I sit on one end of the bench,
raise my head to take on sylvan view
spotting a yellow breasted finch
while remembering this man I knew.
I wonder if he sees this too.

There you are

Leo Feraco (leoferaco)
Ontario, Canada

the season of warmth, or rather inescapable heat, is pulling near. perhaps we can start there. perhaps i can meet her on the curb like we used to. where i asked her if she needed a drive home and she insisted not.

she wore different lashes then. her hair was full and her presence shadowed mine. i remember calling in a panic, "do you feel the way i feel?"

she could always put a name to it.

she felt sand the same way i felt it. the heat on her skin, not the grain between her fingertips. i learned so much in that time. i admired what i thought was her wisdom. though all words were once wise.

~

there you are. hi. hello. don't run off so soon. i found a note in this little book you carried one night. The name that was signed brought me back to you. it was written in the book you bought to take with you everywhere. to be a writer on the go.

The pages sat empty for years, but watch now how fast they fill. each word written carries with it such weight. the ink of my pen must be thicker than what you used.

i know your pain. it lives with me. i feel your joy, which is much easier to forget. i like to look at your photos. not the ones of you, but the ones you took. i like to discover what felt important then. it was all so romantic, all but what was meant to be.

do you remember me? can you see yourself in me? it's alright if you can't. i don't smile as much in photos like you. but you were just a kid. i know you would hate to hear that. i know in ten years, or even just one, i'll say the same about myself.

just know that i miss you if it counts for anything. and whatever it is: no, it is not your fault.

Five Percent Battery

Carrie Chovan (RoseBlack)
New York, United States

Running off fumes,
choking on smoke.
Sucking exhaustion
through pasty lips.

Engine's down a quart,
burn out,
Dark circles tell all,
who is about to fall.

Mercy lights,
Low battery,
jumper cables ignite.
Knock down, drag out fight.

Encroach and Invade

Aaliyah El-Amin (Tawny023)
Maryland, United States

Mold is an inconspicuous bully
Decomposes reds, yellows, oranges
Blues, and even lime greens
Does not matter its outer shape
Covets the wetness deep inside
Feeds and declares dominance
Nest and festers, spreads
Like vermin and vectors
Permeates and inhibits
Its host hold on to structure
While degrading its bonds
In order to have its way with
Just about any old living thing
A temperamental nuisance
But it's grotesque mold juice
caught the eye of Dr. Fleming
Its usefulness is no other
Than the holy grail
called Penicillin
Which fights viruses that would
Otherwise make human's
procreation unviable and
Their deaths excruciating

My Fireside Confession

Guy Caswell (Geezer)
New York, United States

Sex, sax, and smooth whiskey,
secrets beside the fire.
Warm and sultry brown eyes
looking at me, desire.

The pounding of my blood,
pitched ringing of my ears
Cannot turn me away
playing on all my fears.

Warming a frosted heart,
confessing “I love you,”
There’s nothing left to say,
Hope that you love me too.

Leaving On A Train

Carrie Chovan (RoseBlack)
New York, United States

Destination anywhere,
frozen tears pierce my skin,
as a bitter wind slaps my face.
Much like the memories of you and this place.

Passersby, in ghostly form,
not really here but not really gone.
The train rolls in, like storm clouds in the sky.
I've never been so glad to say goodbye.

The conductor, in his broken down attire,
bids me good day as I board his vessel.
One way ticket to parts unknown,
no turning back once the whistle has blown.

My Bucket List

Clentin Martin (Clentin)
Pennsylvania, United States

I fell in love with a heart so true,
I cherish moments, both old and new.
I learned from failures of the past
I pray these actions will always last

My bucket list as a young man, so vast,
A journey of self-discovery, meant to last.
I chased my dreams with passion and might,
In the pursuit of life, to find the light.

Now that life is closer to the end
My bucket list begins to bend
A list once so big and wide
Now is small but full of pride

I no longer wish for cars or money
I seek love and comfort and a bit of honey
I want to see my family live with success
Free of illness free of stress

Backwards

Caroline Joy Hateley (Carrie)
Perth, Australia

G
All the things that I wanna write
C
Have been written
G
All the songs that I wanna sing
D
Have been sung,
G
All the things that I wanna say
C
Have been said before
D A Em G
All the things that I wanna do have been done.

G
I wanna fly a kite
A
At night instead of day,
C
I wanna drive a big old truck
D
The opposite way
G

I wanna laugh when I'm sad,
C
And cry when I'm happy and gay
D A
I wanna do what no one's done
G
Any other day.

G
I wanna wear all my clothes
A
Wear em all inside out,

C
I wanna be real quiet,
D
When everybody else wants to shout
G
I wanna see the stars
C
When everybody else sees the sun
D
I want my day to end
C G
When everybody else's has begun.

C D
Wouldn't it be weird, wouldn't it be funny and strange

A

If everyone thought like this,

G

Slightly deranged.

Granny Overthere.

Ian Frank Rolf (Alex Tanner)
Isle Of Wight, United Kingdom

When so, so young I had a bear,
Her name was Granny Overthere;
A stranger name could not be found
You've not heard that one I'll be bound.

It came from younger brother Tim
Who, whenever mother asked of him
What did he want with which to play
Would point at Granny and loudly say:

"I want Granny, Granny over there",
She always sat in Father's chair.
Thus it was that she was named
And forever Tim would take the blame.

Romance

Hanh Chau (Hon)
California, United States

Under the moonlight
shadow dance
you and I embrace
in a delightful stage
Share in the language
of romantic sparkle
with the happiness
filled our heart
celebrating the new
beginning of life
This marks the promise
of commitment
from god's grace gift
display of precious exude
with a sense of gratitude
granted from a wish
relish with a joy of blessing
for a final reunion

The unexpected

Manja Stojanovic (Mini)
Nis, Serbia

Falling in love with you
Is the most astonishing thing,
For I never imagined
That eyes so blue
Could captivate me so deeply,
Preoccupying my mind
With your enchanting presence,
Becoming a light
In my dark path,
Warmth
In the coldest winter,
Star
In the night sky
And joy
In sorrow

Christmas Lost and Found

Richard A. Milne (Richard Milne)
Washington, United States

For everyone who has lost their way
realize the promise of Christmas Day
all those feeling crippled by fear
understand you can start life anew
by letting the Lord have you

It's not about colored lights, holly or trees
no matter how beautiful things such as these
not about Santa, presents or snow
it's all about knowing where you'll go
at the appointed time to go home

Never forget the meaning of Christmas
let the truth always be told
above the world one holy night
a glorious star shining bright
led the world to Jesus

Mary:
We have to stop, it's getting late
I'm cold and scared and tired
Joseph it's almost time
this child is coming
I need to get some rest tonight

Joseph:
I know the journey has been hard
and Mary I know everything is new
but we've come this far
by our faith in God
and trust He will see us through

Both:
Father above, thank you Lord
we are humbled you've chosen us
to bring your Son into this world
we'll stand our ground
no matter what comes
and pledge our lives and hearts to you

We celebrate this day, a new beginning
the birth of a Savior
to show us the way to heaven
whatever happens to me and you
we'll have a place with God above
when our time here is through

Magic

Diane Pryor (Lavender)
Indiana, United States

A falling star settled on my rose,
a diamond dipped in velvet clothes.
I dared not touch the pure gift
sent from heaven, so swift,
but let it rest there
in such sweet air
and comply
to my
wish.

Working Mom

Sancha Glasgow-Regis (Merlicka)
New Jersey, United States

I have a new boss
She calls me mom
She tells me what to do
Graveyard shifts, sleepless nights
Always on call too

It's a new job
In An entirely different field
One, where the requirements
I never thought I could fulfill
It's not easy, takes a lot of patience,
A lot of Love and tender care
It may not be a job for everyone
But man, I do love it here!

At times, I do get frustrated
Most times I'm exhausted
But the benefits are worthwhile
The pay isn't necessarily what you'd expect
But it's definitely worth the time.

Three Forks

Willian Lynn (Willian Lynn)
Idaho, United States

The Corps of Discovery was born
The year was eighteen zero four,
To find a way to Pacific waters
From St. Lewis they would explore.

The famed expedition to map the West
Led by Lewis and companion Clark,
New discoveries were vast and plenty
Each mapped a unique historic mark.

A Shoshoni girl helped guide them
Through tribal lands of sage and pine,
In Montana they looked in wonder
At three waters they would define.

All three waters soon bore new titles
Indigenous names would just not do,
These newly minted waters joined;
From there the Missouri river grew.

The wide Missouri River proudly flowing
Twenty three hundred miles of thirsty land,
Seven states would know it's precious gifts
Across parched plains this river spanned.

Some would call it the "Big Muddy"
While towards St. Louis it would flow,
It would join the mighty Mississippi
Rolling towards the Gulf of Mexico.

Just one of many wonders found
On the journey to map the West,
Gifts to a growing hope filled nation
Thanks to pioneers that met the test.

Ramming Speed

C.M. Mattison (Candlewitch)
Wisconsin, United States

Unfortunately, the swing sets and
Softball field were down hill from school.
Where daily dramas were played out
under the eyes of an appointed fool.

A pop fly ended our turns at bat
deciding the ending of this game.
We gathered up our softball gear to go
back up to school, like any day, the same.

I was the last kid to dust off and go,
I spotted Carlotta Forbes, up mid hill.
A boulder in a dress blocking me in my path
It was assured one of us would take a spill...

This girl was nuts and a big bully slob
last week she drove a pencil through sis's hand...
There she stood, planted, trying to stare me down
nothing to it but to show her my personal sand.

Getting up that long dirt hill was a must
Carlotta stood, mocking me for a skinny twerp.
Something came over me, I was no longer afraid
I readied myself to go up and settle this Jerk.

Tucking my neck and shoulders, lowering my head
gathering my legs under me I took off like a shot,
barreling up that hill. picking up speed all the way
she was just a target, I was feeling so very 'hot'

I slammed into her like a wrecking ball hits a wall
She went down with a thud, her face a bright red blank.
Sitting there trying to catch her breath again
her face scrunched up as her pride and bluster sank!

I reclaimed my air with longer and longer breaths
then it hit me just what I had done, and what I would do
"never threaten me or my sister again, or you will hurt"
looking up at me, I saw hatred growing, glowing anew!

The Last ring

Ashley Sarath (Jokerface82)
Liverpool, United Kingdom

Blood Detonated out from
my cheeks
in an splatter to the chipped

creamed wall.
The backhand print mark stung
my jaw.

It made my legs weaken fall.
Knocking the
Dial a phone pinging, spinning
to the floor.

The snaked rubber phone wire
fastened around

my neck. A necklace of death
.I'm gasping
for air.
Its demonic shadow grows
over me. It
looks with Sunken dead
eyes at my new

perplexion Im left with. A
sinister grin
breaks
its withdrawn boned face

to a curve of mischievous
delight as
it slowly
stumbles away.

Agony

David Grigorian (David Grigorian)
Colorado, United States

Pain.
I must see you,
And feel your touch,
Taste you,
I need to smell you,

Pain.
Embrace me
Consume me,
I crave you,
In my flesh and bones,
I need to know you.

Pain,
Crush my mind,
Burn my heart,
Drown my soul,
Mold me,
Into you.

Life is What You Are

Ian Frank Rolf (Alex Tanner)
Isle of Wight, United Kingdom

There's a time to go back to live life again,
Let the boy who was fearless be reborn just the same;
Command the old man who grumbles and moans
Of the aches and the pains that torment his old bones.

Ride his bike one more time, no brakes, hands free,
Skate winter's froze pond where he knows not to be,
Go down to the river for frogs, newts, dragonfly,
Climb gnarled oaks so tall they caress azure sky.

Boot footballs, play rugby in fields full of mud.
Wash knees in ice water to clean off the blood
From kicks and from falls but never no pain
Just laughter as into the fray once again.

No laptops, no mobiles perhaps no tv,
But they were not wanted this boy he was free.
Free from an age of want yet to come
To go where he pleases till hungry then home.

From dawn until dusk he was out all around,
With his numerous pals no trouble was found,
Nor was it sought, just laughter and fun
Or maybe some girls as adolescence begun.

The old man sits straight and a smile lights his face
He'll do what he can and if he seems a disgrace?
A silly old sod who ought to know better,
By God! life's for living, he'll show he's no quitter.

Shadows that haunt my thoughts

Fortune Ezekiel Monaheng Motsabi (Headless Two Face Meridian)
Free State, South Africa

Juggling the jugular of jargon from the golden jar gone per sip, intentioned gorged by percipitation,
I stroll through verbal synergies for veracity sived through similies assimilated in receding patience,

Firmly fermented by infirmities which affirm the t's and q's that bear an open scar on my Virgo aura,
All round the fauna of my foraminiferas petal dichotomy disguised as monologs penned as orals.

Was Niztchie too quick to apply for the presumption of death?
Has life become nothing more than just a labyrinth dejavu of consumption of breath?

Scourged by scorching scoff, ameliorated by a million ratings milled beyond a mileu raided,
Words, sound power breeds manifestation materializing immediate familiar blatant...

Cause and effect coarsen affect while soaking dry spells with dyslexic illiterate pen handling.

Who begs to differ when the essence of individualism is just the foundation of soliloques they panhandling?

And, the mirage is just a reflection of shadows that haunt my thoughts,
For when the pen is a fragile cliche... what's mightier than the sword?

Mum... You and I

Rula Younis Ali Hijazi (Rula)
Amman, Jordan

Together we witnessed time ebbs and tides:
we went through ups, we went through downs,
yet luckily we got each other's sides,
you and I, you and I.

Together, unwillingly, we grew old,
with devestating wrinkles, and white hair.
We both raised families, yet we're still bold
You and I, you and I.

Together we laughed, together we cried:
I uplifted your spirits, you got my tears wiped,
we stayed together, side by side,
You and, I you and I.

Together we lived for worse and better,
until Alzheimer's stole you, my bank of love,
although you promised to stay forever
You and I, you and I.

A Cruel Joke

C.M. Mattison (Candlewitch)
Wisconsin, United States

He was wild and adventurous.
A Lothario of great note
discharged from the U.S. Navy,
finding land legs, just off the boat.

Feeling freedom for the first time
from shores of Viet Nam, now home.
Fancy for the neighbors daughter,
this bad cat was out on the roam!

Dating Jan for a month of days
without explanation, he stopped
found another who turned his head
so, by the wayside she was dropped.

Distressed, Jan told him of her plight
He said it was not "His" baby,
smirk, "Why are you not on the pill?"
"It is your own doing, Maybe?"

Taking his dog Blatz to the lake,
scope the scene for girls on the beach
they would run up, give Blatz a pat
well behaved, not needing a leash.

Well trained he stayed by his master
whose eyes found a goal in his range.
Blatz ran ahead with wagging tail
licking faces, as an exchange.

Jerry with Blatz, made connection
smoking on a hash pipe, he sneezed
Blatz sniffed around Mary a bit
then Lifting up his leg, he peed!

Poor Mary with a wet back cried!
Jerry laughed, gave her a poke.
Her eyes glittering her rebuke...
"Too bad you're a big cruel joke!"

A Tribute To A Hero

Olabisi Joshua Oyetunji (Mr joghe)
Osun, Nigeria

The guard that attended to us
Stood in combat to defend us
In death's dark desert wild
Where delight abate
I've missed him like a music.

Through dust of conflict and battle flame
His knightly virtue proved
His memory hallowed in the land he loved
Where death is sitting
All skill, knowledge and powers
And the smile upon his cheerful faces
I've missed him like a music.

By day and night
To bear the people in his heart
His children sang his songs:
In fields so broad
Some duties may fulfil
And I will ask for no reward
Except to serve thee.
From East and West their voices sweetly blended
With the souls he loved.

Mr. Barman

Aaliyah El-Amin (Tawny023)
Maryland, United States

Hey, Mr Barman
Pour me another round
Stop yanking my chain
Why don't you make it a double

It's tomorrow that doesn't matter
Today I just want to get under
It's the yesterday that lingers
Causes me a great amount of pain

Let this one drink make me numb
No longer even notice the rain
Let my troubles drown in peace
Confided in my glass
dwells my happy place
Imbibe in a fancy night cap

Mr. Bar man, my only confidant
If truth be told I'm not sure I will
make it until the neon light flickers
On this bar stool is the only time
I can see this darn clearly
Let the clock strike midnight
just as long as I am surrounded

by all the accoutrements from
an empty bottle

Drifting Clouds

Boikobo Ace Swantalala (Trail)
Gaborone, Botswana

The sun rises a little earlier each day
And each day is brighter than the last
On evenings I walk out to see the sunset
And I walk back with a rested soul

I've tried to be more sincere with myself
To hold my own hand
As I walk through the darkness
To sing to myself once in a while
So that I can hear a voice
Of someone who loves me

It hasn't been an easy ride
But the clouds are coming back from the south now
And with each wave I get a feeling
That it's all going to be alright

I'm waiting for the first rains of the season
Hoping that just maybe
The heavy part of my soul
Will be washed clean
And I can smile again
Even if it's just for a while

I carry a weight in my heart
But when the breeze blows, I look up
I am stunned by the majesty of the clouds
And of the moon, and the stars
This, I think
Is how I survived for so long

Falling For My Therapist

C.M. Mattison (Candlewitch)
Wisconsin, United States

In this place of dank, dark cold
brought on by despondency,
misery of matters murky and old.

History of abuses buried deep,
with gentle fingers, he guides...
dimming lights, bidding me sleep.

Hearing his soft mellow tones,
I feel my consciousnesses drift
to a time of pubescent woes and moans.

His voice is the anchor tethering me
to past present and future,
where I find answers to be.

He hears me when I'm speaking
Without judgement he is clear
almost magick, knowing what I am seeking.

How could I not feel such sheer enchantment
for this strong guide of lost souls,
this wielder of enhancements?

First Ride

Guy Caswell (Geezer)
New York, United States

A warm Spring day, and Mikey sat grinning
"I've found just the thing for you."
He had a smile and a way of winning
with stuff he wanted to do.

Downstairs in the cellar, cool and damp
door open to the backyard,
We went in to peer at Mikey's camp
and at first, seeing's too hard.

But then a shape; of blue paint and chrome
emerging from the gloom
A dream, a chance for me to roam
a bicycle in the room!

It just needs some fixing up yet
the chain is rusted and it's froze
but I know how to free it, I'll bet
I've done a couple of those.

You want to help me fix your ride?
"My ride? I asked, he said "Yes
I'd like a partner at my side"
I agreed, and said I'd do my best

We wrenched and tightened spokes and stuff
patched tubes and pumped them up.
I skinned my knuckles, but I did get tough
we drank kool-aid from plastic cups.

I was nervous, astride the polished seat
First time, I'm gonna fall...
"Relax, says Mikey, you've got this beat
have confidence, that's all.

I went straight down, old Summit Ave
turned around and rode back home
best first ride, I will ever have
And me and Mikey, free to roam.

Hymn of the Bees

Rula Younis Ali Hijazi (Rula)
Amman, Jordan

A goodly morning busy bees,
What's for honey, if you please?
Have you sucked the flowers' juice,
Or hummed to them, tender coos?

Bet you hummed in harmony,
Sang the morning's symphony.
Now it's butter that I need,
Jar of milk , for a perfect heed.

Filled with sweets, up to the brim,
Me and you, singing a hymn.
Lavish to set the rest of the day,
Free and funny all the way.

Archeology

Emma Gagnon (Hippiemoon)
Maine, United States

Years from now,
We will be dead and buried.
Your laugh nothing more than
A whisper in the wind,
A breeze carrying off dandelion wishes.

Our headstones will rest together,
Aging together, as we did in life.
Tears from our loved ones will mix with rain
And our memory will fade with the engravings.

And years from now,
We're forgotten by everyone but the Earth.
They will dig our bodies up
And find our bones entwined in each other's arms.

Wood-smoke

C.M. Mattison (Candlewitch)
Wisconsin, United States

We mellowed...
reclining by the camp fire
after a day of splashing,
swimming, and water games.

I shivered as
evening came in to surround us
with a cooling breeze.
Your fisherman knit sweater
you placed about my shoulders,
staved off a slight chill.

Your glittering orbs
held me intoxicated.
As I felt the last of
the sun's rays
leach out of the sand

Quietly exchanging daydreams,
I noticed, wood-smoke, was
the color of your smiling eyes!

Disambiguation

Dipak Sen (Sen99)
Nottingham, United Kingdom

When sinking in the mire
Water muddy with confusion
Meaning disappears into a black swamp
Redundant words drown in brain fog
Uncertain ground too soft to stand on

When you struggle with meaning
Look at a loved one's face
Study their facial muscles
Lips pursed, the nose upturned
The eyes have it,
The smile knows it.

Don't look for a clear explanation
Instead try anti disambiguation
And if you know what that means
Then climb a mountain of baked beans
All those 57 varieties,
Each one the same bloody bean!

Our Family Feud

C.M. Mattison (Candlewitch)
Wisconsin, United States

When we were young,
lines had been drawn.
Less a friendly battle
than an all-out war.
It was always them
against us...
me (little Honey-Girl)
and our Dad, against
mom-Norma, Kathryn and Coral,
with black cowboy hats.
Blazing guns drawn
from toy holsters.
Something changed;
shifted...
When She hit him
with a frying pan,
I could see in Her eyes
the hate and anger growing.
I think he saw it too...
I saw the pain in his eyes
That is why he arrived
later and later each night,

until he came back not at all...

To Unlove You

Kristen Hardigree (Kristen H.)
Georgia, United States

I'm learning how
To unlove you

It hurts worse than loving you,
Knowing you don't love me back.

Cage of cards

Hayden McCain (Edward nigma)
Virginia, United States

Chaotically clustered
cage of
cards covering
all
cynically silent
sides of life
plainly plastered
before my
persistently passing
presence of
the present day.
Thoughtlessly thrashing
out the leisurely
overlapping lanes
of possibilities
prancing through
the pressuring palms
of probability.
With a single stern stomp
taking back the cross
mask of control.
There steadily
stumbled down
the obliquely built

walls of ambiguity
freely falling at
my frivolously
fleeting feet.
Vigorously revealing
the vaguely vapid
valley of victorious
vultures who
persistently preys
upon the weak
minded ones
who decisively numb
themselves within naivety .
But still
I walk forth
ahead through
the foreboding facade
of fear
lying before me.

Moth to a Flame

Dipak Sen (Sen99)
Nottingham, United Kingdom

She is like a naked flame starved of oxygen.
White hot but almost exhausted,
Weary like a candle at the end of its life.

I'm a blind, deranged moth
Excited to be flying towards her cold fire,
Eager to be engulfed by her,
Hypnotized and confused by one last flicker of light.

A moth has no mouth
Still, I wanted to lick her flame,
One last taste of her tongue,
A final kiss before extinction.

Just before I reached her, she blew out,
Extinguished by a winter wind
Her soot and ashes
Were just dead memories of a failed love.

Higher and Higher

Shelby Pryor (Shelby Pryor)
Tennessee, United States

I've been on my back lately
I haven't tried getting up
I've embraced the tears
But enough is enough

I won't just get up now
I'll rise like a Phoenix
Shaking the ashes off
The life that I'll fix

I will not be passive
It is time to ravage
The fear inside me
I'll attack like a savage

Wipe the blood from my lip
Dust the dirt off my hands
For victory belongs to the one
Who runs, not who stands

Fire comsumes my heart
Burning up all the pain
You might have crushed me
But it was not in vain

What destroys the others
Will not mar my skin
The scars are finally fading
My thread no longer thin

So watch my eyes ignite
Watch my steps shift
I'll treat my life not as
As a curse but a gift

I am done holding back
Living like a caged-up lion
I will keep getting up
When it feels like I'm dyin'

So give me back the pen
Only I can write my story
Every drop of blood spilled
Is another step towards glory

You can deliver a steep uppercut
But I'm a last round fighter
Even with you pushing me down
I keep flying Higher and Higher

We're almost there for it

Rula Younis Ali Hijazi (Rula)
Amman, Jordan

"Where do dreams hide?" Once asked my child
"Behind the stars, I've always replied."
"The dreams hide, where stars reside."
" Once asked my child, where do dreams hide."

Where dreams reside, there shines a light,
With few brave steps , the way we'll find
Let's find the way where stars shine bright
There shines a light where dreams reside.

We aren't there yet, few steps are left,
to reach the dream we got to set
unfurl the dream, never forget
few steps are left, we aren't there yet

With hearts so fit, we're there for it.
A dream we oft longed out to get
Bit after bit, we'll never quit
We're there for it with hearts so fit.

My Heart, My Heaven

Kevin Alfred Devereux (Izzi Reinier)
Victoria, Australia

With my eyes i can touch the universe
With my heart could i change the world
With my wisdom i can form an opinion
And with my hands could i sculpture a form.

With my family i can create a community
With my faith could the world change me
With my values i can judge impartially
And with my love ,can i be fairly judged

With my honour i can defend all goodness
With my observances can i find the truth
With mankind in perfect harmony
And with blessings to a greater god go i

Fooled Again

Guy Caswell (Geezer)
New York, United States

Warm breeze dances with cold winds
round and round they go.
Through the trees, wind whipped thin,
hear them sigh and sough.

Flutterbys and hummingbirds
sipping nectar brews,
carry smells and sexiness,
just like precious jewels.

May will gather her bouquet,
Kiss her brow, my favorite sun,
caress her skin with warmth, I say,
she'll love you when you're done.

It's just a fling, this Springtime thing,
remember what I say,
she'll just run off with Summer again,
on that perfect weather day.

It happens every year, it does.
She fools you every time.
I don't know why you fall for it.
but it makes for such good rhyme.

Echoes

Boikobo Ace Swantalala (Trail)
Gaborone, Botswana

Once there was a man
Who wrote beautiful music
He wrote the music because he was sad
He was sad because he was all alone

But he was noticed for his music
He ended up being loved for it
And in being loved
He lost his sadness
And his music soon after

Enchantress

Ian Frank Rolf (Alex Tanner)
Isle Of Wight, United Kingdom

Her laugh is soft, it flutters
As butterfly wings in spring.
Her dark eyes wide, they sparkle
As the purest diamond ring.

She is the sweetest angel
That any man could know;
Yet deep within her ageless soul
Dark vices wrought men woe.

She loves to woo and taunt them,
To lead them on with guile,
To bring them pain and misery
Bestowed with lasvicious smile.

Her pleasure is to lure them
Bind them helpless then,
As victim snared in spider's web
Inflict pleasure close to pain.

With nails as sharp as cut throats
She scores their bodies deep,
She sucks the bloodied wounds
Enough to make them weep,

As all the while her laughter
Soft, flutters round the cell;
She coos words of endearment,
They writhe in self made hell.

No man who lusts is safe from her
She knows their weakest links,
And like the spider hunting prey
Destroys them in a wink.

Too Good to Be True

Paula Frew (Punkyfrewster)
Ohio, United States

In my mind, it was bliss
day in and day out
until the day it ended.

In the rearview mirror,
I saw signs:
far-off gazes to nowhere
as we ate dinner
and stalled conversations
about your day.

All the bliss aside,
our love was just
too good to be true.

Haunting Me

Guy Caswell (Geezer)
New York, United States

Unexplained whispers
creaking in the floors
Ghostly sighs and rattles
of the knobs upon the doors

Could it be the house is weary?
All these lives it's had to bear
from dancing in the bedroom
to shrieking, pulling hair

I think that I can hear them,
thoughts telling me to listen
I've heard them many nights
alone, out in the kitchen

The 'fridge' grumbles to itself
as I shut the open door
"I just want a sandwich,
that and nothing more"

But here they come again,
little paws with nails
scratching on the tiles
I almost see their wagging tails

The old lady had two tiny dogs
they ruled the yard out there
She yelled at them, to "Get those squirrels"
they looked at her, like where?

Settle down, motley-crew
I'm burning midnight oil
I'm writing stories here
please, be quiet while I toil

My tea got cold, while I worked
Good night, my ghostly friends
there be word limits here, make it short
because this is where it ends.

In Another Life I Live Bravely

Nora VanDerMeid (MermaidMaster)
New York, United States

I want to live in the tallest apartment in New
York City, and peer my gaping eyes through
my window to see only dancing beetles below.

I will wear expensive feathers and furs, I'll
dance with strangers, and I'll party for a while
with headliners after sold-out shows.

I'll walk the streets wearing only perfume and
watch men stand agape as I strut past, too awed
at my nakedness proud and aglow.

I'll rebel and I'll wail and I'll cry out,
"Change will come! Justice will prevail!"
And I won't shut up until Change comes and goes.

I'll play poker with CEO's, and kiss strange men in taxis,
and spin through the nights like a globe on its axis;
to live with honeyed hi's! And never with lows.

I'll do pilates and yoga, drink only red wine,
and I won't dwell on the men who used to be mine.

I'll live fast and so furiously young,
and I'll die gentle, soft and divine.

Whistle Stop Grove

Kevin Alfred Devereux (Izzi Reinier)
Victoria, Australia

There's A Shady Grove Where The Morning Sun Gives Birth, 'Neath The Boughs Of A Sycamore Tree Where It Teases Mother Earth,

Where The Dew Drops Glisten On To The Grassy Verge And The Ants In Frantic Cycle,
As To Their Lives Purposeful Worth,

"Old Shep " Walks By As To Survey His Dominion, This Empire Soon To Awaken To His Heirs Timely Arrival,

His Majestic Prescence In This Perfect Morning Glory, Wary Of Unwelcome Foe's And Un witting Rivals,

The Breeze Freshens Presently The Dry Leaves Dance And Dive , Which Only Haltens Momentarily , To Their Decay In Endless Passage,

Steady Old Snail Taking Care As He Ambles , He's Crossed Paths Once Before When Those Ants Have Turned Savage,

The Sun Hides Behind A Pillow Of White , Then Returns To Find The Master, Passing By In His Carriage,

He Whistles "Old Shep" As The Lambs Jump And Frolic, Too Young To Know Danger , Innocent Hearts Filled With Courage,

Wiley Brown Fox Couches Down High Up On The Ridge , His Day Full Of Promise , To His Quarry's Last Regret,

There's A Secret Shady Grove Hidden Out Here Amongst The Bramble, Coverts The Sunrays And The Shadows Against All New Comers Debt...

To Those Who Walked

Diane Pryor (Lavender)
Indiana, United States

I hope you have a quiet day,
a kissing breeze,
sweet hours at ease
planting flowers, if you please,
and nothing there to rip it all away.
I hope you have that day.

I pray you have a gentle night,
under stars so deep
they soothe and keep
your soft breath flowing as you sleep
beneath the crescent moon and her earthlight.
I pray you have that night.

And may your memories be amended
to blissful skies and green earth, so splendid
that they embrace you when you close your eyes.
May this be the rich life you come to realize.

To those who walked through the blood of yesternight,
I hope for you this day. I pray for you this night.

Parallel

Emma Gagnon (Hippiemoon)
Maine, United States

There's a universe where I never met you,
Where your hands never ran across my skin.
We never kissed in the backseat of my parents' car,
Faces flushed from the thrill.

Maybe in this universe,
We were on opposite ends of the earth.
My night was your day.
Where I saw a sunset, you saw a sunrise.
Both skies being painted, but with different brushes.

Or maybe we were next door neighbors
But never ran across each other.
I would hear your lawnmower
And your snowblower
And see your dogs running in the yard
Over my white picket fence that separates us,
But I would never see you.

I would wonder about the life you lead.
Hypothetical you, of course, because it's easy to build a life with someone you never met.

But in this universe,
I knew you
And I loved you
As much as a girl can love a boy who doesn't love her enough.

Maybe in a different universe
We will live parallel.
Close enough,
But never to meet.
The scars left on my soul will heal
If they carry over from another world.

And I will love someone
But he will not be you
Because in another universe
I am too smart to be hurt by you.

Lovers Dance

Ian Frank Rolf (Alex Tanner)
Isle Of Wight, United Kingdom

They skip, they leap, they dance, they fly
Till on their lovers breast they lie,
Up again once more they prance
You may not give a second glance.

As Autumn into Winter flows
Winds pick up and start to blow,
Choose myriad colours from the trees
And start the ball of Autumn leaves.

Do you not watch them as they fly?
From one love to another hie,
While we dance life's eternal waltz
Then like the leaves we end the course.

After school treat

John Leslie Boydstun (Leslie)
Utah, United States

Mom would make them,
bake them up sweet!
They were supposed to be
the whole families treat?
I'd stand right beside her
stealing spoonfuls of batter.
When I was a kid
well, not much else mattered!
She'd criss cross the tops
and bake them together.
By the time they were finished
the aroma had gathered,
straight up in our nostrils
from off of the platter.
We'd run to the table
and take off our ball caps,
to eat them with milk
and take a long nap!

Neo Gems

A Walk With You

Michael Anthony McPeek (Micheal Anthony)
California, United States

We invited the sun to join us.
To come out from behind that sullen cloud
and share with us late in the morning.

With amber light breaking through,
in tow as company for the day,
our hands were together and warmed
but not by the busy sun.

No offense was taken,
our yellow star assured us,
as we walked between the shadows
being painted all around us.

Wildfires

C.M. Mattison (Candlewitch)
Wisconsin, United States

your life,
was like a night game
played out in the rain...

your love,
like fabled moths
flying to the flame...

your heart,
like a songbird
trapped in a gilded cage...

your soul,
a wounded animal
twisted in pain and rage...

just your precious being
setting both our souls afire
touching and in reach...

your eyes, spoke to me
of the tiniest desire,
as you ran out of speech...

The same prevalent path

Hayden McCain (Edward nigma)
Virginia, United States

Forever falling
down the
same appalling
path . pathed
in passion
pinched with pain
ruefully wrapped
in rage . Still
Relentlessly rowing
through its
enraging river
of wrath.

Vestiges

Kevin Bloor (Blue-eyed Bolla)
Buxton, United Kingdom

Left here in land of hill and peak,
where storms of sorrow slyly seek
to weary me and weigh me down:
I never chose this tortured town!

These song birds, blown upon the wing,
they squawk and sway, but rarely sing.
Since bleakness blinds them, blinds me too:
turns sapphire skies to black from blue.

Left here to age, while clouds race by,
I wait, as one by one they die:
those vestiges of youthful dreams
that seep away like sea-bound streams.

To Love

Okpanachi Shadrach Adakole (Sheddie)
Lagos, Nigeria

To love like the golden sun,
Showering care on the weakened moon,
Two to one, everyone comes alive,
Together we breathe, every tear, every run,
To love for love, that's the way to love.

To love like the rain,
Kissing every face and name, no matter the case,
Everything knowing its cause, stainless, pure,
Beauty blossoms in hearts, not visions, nor gain,
To love for love, that's the miracle of love.

To love like mother earth,
Embracing laughter, lashes, success, struggles,
Everyone equal, a ladder for a brother,
In darkness, hope remains alive, blessed,
To love for love, that's the only cure.

To love like a life in love,
Always bringing reasons to smile, enjoying every moment,
Good people, great times, happy souls, happy memories,
Loving and being loved in return, bliss rising above,
To love for love, that's a dream come true.

Spring chill

Ashley Sarath (Jokerface82)
Liverpool, United Kingdom

Fresh mint green lawns
A black silk feathered bird
hopping On delicate
springs

Tangerine beaked bill
seeking out it's next meal

Cloud birds on wings
of symphony travelling
from the pop stars of the
trees

filling into the dome of
Electric blue skies a
bone warming blissfulness.

Bright blades of golden
sunshine massaging
the backs of peaceful
gardens.

monk droning bees
filling the buttery rays.

palettes of sweltering
oranges and fiery reds
and burning yellow

flowers

Colours

Caroline Joy Hateley (Carrie)
Perth, Australia

Green is the colour
Of the deep dark sea
Blue is the feeling
Deep within me

Red is the colour
Of the red sky at night
Yellow is the colour
Of the sun so bright

Black is the colour
Of a cave, deep and dark
Brown is the colour
Of an old trees bark

Grey is the colour
Of the socks I have on
One day these colours
In my heart will belong

Ha! Ha! Ha!
They're laughing at me
So I'll keep on thinking
Of trying to be free

Two, three, four
They're locking my door
Six, seven, eight
It's not even late
I wish I was a sparrow
Into the sun I'd fly
I wish I was a kookaburra,
whose laugh is strong but shy

Sunflower

Manja Stojanovic (Mini)
Nis, Serbia

You remind me of the sun
You illuminate and sheen
You warm my heart
You delight me
So incredibly
in such way that
I'm blinded by you
But i can't desist looking
Im a sunflower
The sun is the reason
Why i kept my body and soul together
But the sun
Paid no attention
To a trivial thing like me

Somehow

Zachary Stabb (Zach)
Montreal, Canada

somehow you're everywhere
you're in the street lights
that bring life to the dark
you're in the leaves of a sycamore
in an evergreen kind of way
the birds look to you for help
in singing the sweetest songs
at night the Aurora searches
for it's lost colour in your eyes
i longed for that light, now I've found it
and somehow
its more beautiful than I could've imagined

To Be Brave Is To Live

Anna Severchuk (Anna Severchuk)
Odessa, Ukraine

In the hustle and bustle of everyday strife,
There are moments that bring a touch of life,
Small but beautiful, they sparkle and gleam,
Making our existence a wondrous dream.
A gentle breeze on a warm summer's day,
Caressing our skin as we laugh and play,
The sound of raindrops tapping on the roof,
A lullaby that whispers with a soothing truth.
A smile from a stranger passing us by,
A simple gesture that makes our spirits fly,
A heartfelt conversation, shared with a friend,
Words that uplift and help us mend.
In these small moments, life finds its grace,
A reminder that joy can be found in any place.

Tulips of Love

Aaliyah El-Amin (Tawny023)
Maryland, United States

Love in spring season
Prettier than all others
Vibrantly alive

So giddy within
Teeming delight more blissful
Rejoicing splendor

Enthralled by its bloom
Curious yet Courageous
Spring is eternal

To Walk Beneath Aspens

Stan Holliday (Scribbler)
South Carolina, United States

I always thought I'd go out west
during the early weeks of fall
and roam Rocky Mountains in a quest
for antelope, mule deer, elk and all.

But I must wait 'till school is done
my priorities were clear and set.
There's no hunting under summer's sun.
My time to go was not here yet.

And still I dreamed of aspen's gold
but there was work that must be done
building a business, truth be told
along with marriage and first son.

Oh, there was time but always scattered
never enough for a trip there.
I had to do what really mattered
a life to make and love to share.

Even so, whenever fall turned cold
I'd dream of scattered mountain meadows
outlined by aspen leaves of gold
where I'd walk among the mottled shadows.

Things came up as is their way
building a home for sons and wife
all things to be done day to day
as passing time became a life.

Even while hunting southern deer
amid maple, oak and poplar trees
in familiar forests near and dear
I'd dream of aspens quaking in the breeze.

But there was always this or that
until now at last my window's passed.
I'm too lame, too old and way too fat.
Those mountain views will go un-glassed.

I long yet to walk in scattered trees
of straight burnished aspens in the fall
while listening to the distant tease
of a far off elk's high haunting call.

Bees

Katy Louise Barrass (Katy Louise)
Bridgend, United Kingdom

Soft breeze
carrying fat bees.
Their bums dusted in pollen,
leaving yellow blobs on cotton
as the laundry waves at passers by.

Butterfly Missives

Horacio Chávez (Horacio)
New Mexico, United States

As we remained on a flight from Kansas City
Destined for St. Louis
A group of students quietly came aboard
At first there was nothing amiss
Soon I realized they were deaf
No words but an occasional off-key chortle

What came next were hands floating
Butterfly messages softly, fluidly
At the speed of light
Hands and fingers fluttered
Like Monarchs migrating to
Their appointed destination

Heads and bodies turning and twisting
Like quakies in the wind
Leafy wings flittering
Bursts of gold and green
Silently signaling encrypted notes
In their secret semaphore

A Holy Plea

Apostolos Anagnostopoulos (Paul)
New York, United States

Lord,Words seem
To have
Evacuated

Emotions
Kidnapped my,
Smile
No ransom note
Just, a big
I told you so

They say,
Talking to you
Will save my soul
From hitting
The concrete

I was informed
That you
Know what
Invades my mind

Right now,
My faith

Is taking jabs
To the stomach

Somehow it
Endures,
It never
Hits the
Snooze button

No, it holds me
As if it was
Following orders
From you

I know I don't call
Barely pray
Still may I ask
For you
To send faith
To every soul,
That wrestles
A grief that
Kills slowly

If you need some
Take mine
And pour it in
The hearts

That would
Yell help
If they could

If I could make
These stanzas
Into a smile
For sad faces

I would write until
My fingers fell off
Then I would
Find the highest
Building and
Scream it

All I can do is
Fill pages
With words
That will never
Heal their pain

I still know
You have the final say
Therefore may
Your will be done

Venus Tree

Dipak Sen (Sen99)
Nottingham, United Kingdom

Standing here for decades
On one wooden leg
A native English species,
An old grey oak.
Its naked bark bleached,
Ashen white like alabaster.

She is a nameless uncarved block
Unyielding and proud,
Exposed to the elements.
Wind and weather beaten
An organic body of life,
Her beauty gaunt and raw.

Striking to an admirer's eye,
Picture perfect from a distance,
A stone sculpture, arms cut down to stumps.

Like some replica of a classical statue
From an ancient age,
Nature's beauty,
A timeless art.

If This Tender Morning

C.M. Mattison (Candlewitch)
Wisconsin, United States

...were a beatific elaborate costume,
I would raise my arms, don it like a gown.
Its design by Mother Nature's purity
sundry autumn leaves plucked from the ground.

With the arrival of Autumn's graceful face,
there's a kind of peace I find divine.
To touch within, a sweet well-spring of grace
blessed once again, by nature sublime.

Wandering eyes

Hayden McCain (Edward nigma)
Virginia, United States

Wistful wandering eyes
scattering across
the cool colorless
cloud filled skies.
Desperately
digging through
its shallow
shades of white
in search
for some subtle
sight of light.

Adopting At Our Age

Ray Miller (Ray Miller)
Worcestershire, United Kingdom

This poem went places that it shouldn't have gone
in the beer tent listening to a jazz ensemble,
who came on after the dance band
and are suffering by comparison.
I'm trying to examine the difference between
flute solos and close harmonies,
between thrown together and tightly knit,
being here for themselves or the audience.
I'm with two of my grown-up daughters
and my wife is with the foster kids
watching Maleficent at the cinema.
I'm digging the songs my dad used to sing
and thinking of the time that children thieve
and all the things we won't achieve,
like learning how to jive and lindy hop.
I'm piling up reasons we shouldn't adopt.

Because flowers aren't supposed to bloom in winter.
It looked different in December
when the dark days served to blinker us
and we fought our tiny Christmas tree corner.
It was sisters skipping arm in arm
in the absence of a sibling assessment
by the Solomons at Social Services,

their swords discreetly kept from sight.
It was the country lurching to the right
and a butterfly wish to flap my wings
and make waves in some unsafeguarded centre,
feeling that we'd let them down
if we didn't move heaven and earth
to keep them together.

Now summer shines a bulb in our faces
and mine has started to crack.
It's when the social worker asked
if we think we'll ever harbour some resentment;
it's the sports day when the Downs' Syndrome
trailed in a long way last and was clapped
all the way up the finishing straight,
while I kept my hands firmly in my pocket,
like refusing to stand for the National Anthem;
It's the medical when the doctor found
there's something not quite right with my heart.
Next week they're investigating further.
I felt a little lightening, the hint of a reprieve,
but probably it's no more than a murmur

.

.

.

.

The Memories of Water

Ruby Lord (Ruby Lord)
South Summerset, United Kingdom

Water never forgets,
each drop a fragment of what once was.
Rivers carved through stone recalling glaciers,
oceans echo the songs of long-gone whales.

Rain falls, heavy with stories,
whispering of mountains it nurtured,
and deserts it dared to cross.
It pools in lakes, holding reflections for centuries.

A single droplet clings to a leaf,
remembering the storm it survived,
the clouds it left behind,
and the roots it will soon embrace.

As it pours into you, surrender to its touch,
an ancient pulse, flowing through your veins.
We are all vessels of water and time,
our lives an endless rhythm of ebb and flow.

The water waits, timeless and restless,
its memories shifting with the tides,
tracing the endless cycle
of return.

Loveless

Kevin Bloor (Blue-eyed Bolla)
Buxton, United Kingdom

It's autumn's lonely afternoon,
the sun is sinking slow.
The leaves are bleeding from the trees,
why did she have to go?

The sky is blue between the clouds,
and since she went to roam,
there stands an empty shell of stone
we used to call a home.

It's twilight, so sad stars appear.
Then darkness casts its spell.
Inside the house,
where lovebirds breathed,
I live my Loveless hell.

Take Leave

Enda Patrick Colins (Ziggy)
Roscommon, Ireland

Take leave from City streets
constant illumination head west
through urban sprawl to where
the night sleeps easy

Take time for roads less travelled
those of grass verge and gravel
follow the through-fare walking
along its centered spine

Taking note of the sward what is
there within its keep the hedgerow
along its ditch that forever creeps
to where harvests meadows lay golden

Take heed of your direction remember
my words the landmarks I mentioned
and the turns to take to where I
eagerly await your presence

Take sight of my humble abode
your journey comes to welcome end
open arms a joyful embrace
thoughts exchanged there after.

The Dog and I

Michael Keens (Michael Keens)
Hampshire, United Kingdom

This old bed's so cold it keeps us awake
And the roof, it leaks - when wet it may break.
We don't hear complaints from the rafters
In silence they cry, an absence of laughter.
Despite our struggles, the dog still gets cuddles
We're the best of friends, don't call me his master.
The dog's by my side with his faithful brown eyes
Together we weather the storms and survive.
We walk by the lake, come rain or shine
He searches for rabbits and I long for a time
When we go back to a cabin, that's cosy and dry
Where the sheets are warm and the rafters don't cry.
This is our little world, and we always get by
At our lakeside home, the dog and I

Neopoem Of The Year 2021

Aussieland is Calling

Guy Caswell (Geezer)
New York, United States

I'd like to live down-under
In Aussieland by the sea
With wallabies and waves of thunder
And Eucalyptus trees

The Outback filled with the songs
Of Kookaburra birds
And frog-filled billabongs
Grasslands and kangaroo herds

I'd listen through the night
To Aboriginal didgeridoos
Watch the sun come up bright
Look for spiders in my shoes

Ahhhh, the call of the wild
The Outback calling me
Me, a nature-child
A regular Croc Dundee

Neopoem Of The Year 2022

Time Machine

Gemmna Hesse (Words.unwritten)
Yorkshire, United Kingdom

If I could build a Time machine
I'm not sure where I'd go
A chance to alter memories
Unmeet people that I know

To unsay words I shouldn't have said
And say ones I wish I had
Rewrite each badly written page
Relive days spent with my dad

Unbreak my broken heart
Undoing all damage done
Erasing all the bad times
And relive all the fun

But I can't build a Time machine
So play cards dealt by fate
I don't need to Time travel
To a specific date

I've learnt that Time is precious
So why go back and waste it
Yes my future is unknown

But I can't wait to taste it

Life itself's a time machine
Wherever my destination
I will live each day content
In its subtle variation.

Neopoem Of The Year 2023

Lost Companion

Ian Frank Rolf (Alex Tanner)
Isle Of Wight, United Kingdom

We've walked wild blossom filled meadows,
Bees hummed in verdant grass,
Birds sang in leaf clad hedgerows,
Rabbits fled as we strolled past.

We've walked through winter woodlands
Snow deep upon the path;
Geese took their flight before us
By ponds like crystal glass.

Winter's dawn or Summer's sunset
Together we have been
Inseparable companions
Linked by a common gene.

No more to race through bluebell woods,
No more to frighten hares,
No more to roll in autumn leaves,
No more to hear my cares.

No more to sit in dappled glade
As you lay at my feet,
Your soulful eyes ne'er left my face
You judged not when I speak.

Alone I walk the meadows
The woods in winter too.
And though I walk in silence
I feel your presence through.

Neopoem Of The Year 2024

To Those Who Walked

Diane Pryor (Lavender)
Indiana, United States

I hope you have a quiet day,
a kissing breeze,
sweet hours at ease
planting flowers, if you please,
and nothing there to rip it all away.
I hope you have that day.

I pray you have a gentle night,
under stars so deep
they soothe and keep
your soft breath flowing as you sleep
beneath the crescent moon and her earthlight.
I pray you have that night.

And may your memories be amended
to blissful skies and green earth, so splendid
that they embrace you when you close your eyes.
May this be the rich life you come to realize.

To those who walked through the blood of yesternight,
I hope for you this day. I pray for you this night.